clarity

A Journal for Reflection & Discovery

Katie Caples

Year of the Book
135 Glen Avenue
Glen Rock, PA 17327

ISBN 13: 978-1-945670-94-7
ISBN 10: 1-945670-94-0

INTRODUCTION

Inner clarity is a feeling, a peace of mind that we are moving in a positive, authentic direction. It is a sentiment in our soul and is something we all seek.

My sentiments shifted after welcoming my second daughter. It was subtle at first, and grew louder and stronger with each day. In those wee morning hours of feedings, diaper changes, and baby cuddles, I knew I had reflective work to do to redefine myself.

I started small, jotting down a few bulleted words on the back of random grocery store receipts. The more I created space for internal dialogue, the easier it became. Within a few weeks I had developed a consistent journaling habit. My reflective style evolved as I became more intentional. I began to follow my favorite authors and thought leaders and gained wisdom along the way. I discovered my inner, authentic voice.

Now, a year later, I'm living my dream. I gracefully transitioned from a career that I loved to spend more time with my family and pursue my passions. I'm clear on my priorities and have turned my love for writing into an invigorating business.

As you continue on your journey of reflection and personal growth, I hope this journal both inspires and challenges you. Embrace it as a list keeper, doodle book, spiritual map, or reflective guide.

Slow down, create space, and open your heart as you explore your narrative.

To you, with love.

SHE REMEMBERED
WHO SHE WAS
AND THE GAME CHANGED.

-- LALAH DELIA

I AM:

I AM NOT:

BE VULNERABLE.
GET UNCOMFORTABLE.
BE PRESENT WITH PEOPLE
WITHOUT SACRIFICING
WHO YOU ARE.

- - BRENÉ BROWN

THESE THINGS MAKE ME UNCOMFORTABLE:

O

O

O

O

YOU ARE BRAVER
THAN YOU BELIEVE,
STRONGER THAN YOU SEEM,
AND SMARTER THAN YOU THINK.

-- A. A. MILNE

HOW AM I:

BRAVE?

STRONG?

SMART?

The more
you praise and
celebrate your life,
the more there is in
life to celebrate.

-- Oprah Winfrey

THINGS TO CELEBRATE:

1

2

3

4

5

WHEN THERE IS TOO MUCH, SOMETHING IS MISSING.

-- LEO ROSTEN

WHAT IS TAKING UP SPACE IN MY LIFE?

SURROUND YOURSELF
WITH PEOPLE WHO
BRING JOY AND
GROWTH INTO
YOUR LIFE.

-- BRENDON BURCHARD

THREE PEOPLE WHO BRING ME JOY:

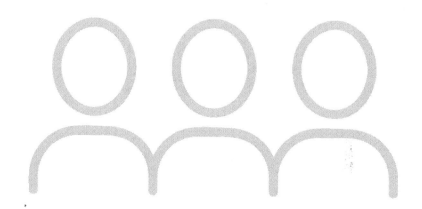

THEY HELP ME GROW BY:

I have no special talents.
I am only **passionately** curious.

-- Albert Einstein

I AM MOST CURIOUS ABOUT:

OUR CALL TO COURAGE
IS TO PROTECT OUR
WILD HEART AGAINST
CONSTANT EVALUATION,
ESPECIALLY OUR OWN.

-- BRENÉ BROWN

♥

POSITIVE WORDS THAT DESCRIBE ME:

TO LIVE
IS THE RAREST
THING IN THE WORLD.

MOST PEOPLE EXIST,
THAT IS ALL.

-- OSCAR WILDE

I PLAN TO LIVE MORE BY:

WHEN I SIMPLY EXIST, I FEEL:

MAKE TIME
THE GIFT IT IS,
BY GIVING IT
TO WHAT REALLY
MATTERS TO YOU.

-- S.C. LOURIE

MY DAILY ROUTINE...

MORNING:

AFTERNOON:

EVENING:

BEFORE YOU RUSH
THROUGH ONE MORE DAY,
SLOW YOUR PACE AND
SAVOR THE MOMENT.

-- ANNE MCCOMBER

I PLEDGE TO SAVOR:

1

2

3

Sometimes
you will never
know the value
of a moment
until it becomes
a memory.

-- Dr. Seuss

MY FAVORITE MEMORY FROM THE WEEK:

The soul always
knows what to do
to heal itself.
The challenge is to
silence the mind.

-- Caroline Myss

WHAT HEALING DOES MY SOUL NEED?

BE RUTHLESS FOR YOUR OWN WELL-BEING.

-- HOLLY BUTCHER

HOW AM I TAKING CARE OF MYSELF?

It always seems impossible
until it's done.

-- Nelson Mandela

WHAT SEEMS IMPOSSIBLE?

WE ARE
WHAT WE
REPEATEDLY
DO.

-- ARISTOTLE

MY BEST HABITS:

MY WORST HABITS:

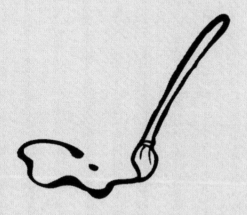

You can't use up
creativity.

The more you use,
the more you have.

-- Maya Angelou

THE LAST TIME I WAS CREATIVE...

Just be yourself.
Let people see the
real, imperfect,
flawed, quirky,
weird, beautiful,
magical person
that you are.

-- Mandy Hale

I AM QUIRKY WHEN:

I AM BEAUTIFUL BECAUSE:

I AM THE MOST MAGICAL:

You gain strength, courage
and confidence by every
experience in which you really
stop to look fear in the face.

-- Eleanor Roosevelt

MY FEARS:

PERFECT IS NEVER.
LIVE NOW.

-- MARCIA ARAMOVICH

I FEEL MOST ALIVE WHEN:

IF YOU DON'T WANT TO BURN OUT,
STOP LIVING LIKE YOU'RE ON FIRE.

-- UNKNOWN

THREE THINGS I WILL SAY "NO" TO:

1

2

3

THE PRIVILEGE OF A
LIFETIME IS BEING
WHO YOU ARE.

-- JOSEPH CAMPBELL

I WANT PEOPLE TO REMEMBER ME FOR...

I WANT TO DO LIFE
- EACH DAY, EACH MOMENT -
LESS ON AUTOPILOT AND
MORE ON PURPOSE.

-- ERICA LAYNE

THESE THINGS FILL ME WITH PURPOSE:

The real difficulty is to
overcome how you think
about yourself.

-- Maya Angelou

WHO DOES MY INNER VOICE SOUND LIKE?

WHAT DOES IT SAY?

I WOULD RATHER OWN LITTLE
AND SEE THE WORLD,
THAN OWN THE WORLD
AND SEE LITTLE OF IT.

-- ALEXANDER SATTLER

TOP THREE PLACES TO VISIT:

Life is a dance between
making it happen and
letting it happen.

-- Arianna Huffington

THE LAST TIME I DANCED...

THE PRESENT MOMENT
IS AN OPPORTUNITY
FOR BRIGHT NEW
BEGINNINGS.

-- GABBY BERNSTEIN

WHAT NEW THING AM I EXCITED ABOUT?

Simplicity,
patience,
compassion.

These three are your
greatest treasures.

-- Lao Tzu

THE REASON(S) I TREASURE...

SIMPLICITY:

PATIENCE:

COMPASSION:

YOU GET IN LIFE
WHAT YOU HAVE
THE COURAGE
TO ASK FOR.

-- OPRAH WINFREY

I HAVE THE COURAGE TO ASK FOR...

EVERY DAY MAY NOT BE GOOD,
BUT THERE IS SOMETHING
GOOD IN EVERY DAY.

-- UNKNOWN

TODAY'S GOOD THINGS ARE:

You can choose
courage
or you can choose
comfort,
but you cannot
choose both.

-- Brené Brown

THE MOST COURAGEOUS PERSON I KNOW:

>

HERE'S WHY:

we are the dreamers of dreams.

-- ROALD DAHL

MY CHILDHOOD DREAMS:

Because when
you stop and
look around,
this life is
pretty amazing.

-- Dr. Seuss

AMAZING THINGS IN MY LIFE:

YOUR MAGIC CAN
MOVE MOUNTAINS

—

RISE UP AND OWN
YOUR POWER.

-- BROOKE HAMPTON

THE MOUNTAINS I'M FACING:

It feels better to do stuff
than to have stuff.

-- James Wallman

STUFF I LOVE TO DO:

WE'RE SO BUSY
WATCHING OUT FOR
WHAT'S JUST AHEAD OF US
THAT WE DON'T
TAKE TIME TO ENJOY
WHERE WE ARE.

-- BILL WATTERSON

I EXPERIENCE JOY WHEN:

SIMPLICITY BOILS
DOWN TO TWO STEPS:
IDENTIFY THE ESSENTIAL.
ELIMINATE THE REST.

-- LEO BABAUTA

MY ESSENTIALS:

Be silly.
Be honest.
Be kind.

-- Ralph Waldo Emerson

I AM SILLY WHEN:

I AM HONEST BECAUSE:

I AM KIND TO:

You don't just luck into things
as much as you'd like to think you do.
You build step by step, whether it's
friendships or opportunities.

-- Barbara Bush

I BUILD FRIENDSHIPS BY:

THE SECRET OF CHANGE IS TO
FOCUS ALL OF YOUR ENERGY,
NOT ON FIGHTING THE OLD,
BUT ON BUILDING THE NEW.

-- SOCRATES

MY FOCUS IS ON BUILDING...

IT'S NOT WHAT YOU
LOOK AT THAT MATTERS,
IT'S WHAT YOU SEE.

-- HENRY DAVID THOREAU

I VALUE:

I CONSISTENTLY PRIORITIZE:

The most valuable gift you can give yourself is the time to nurture the unique spirit that is you.

-- Oprah Winfrey

I WILL NURTURE MY SPIRIT BY:

1

2

3

•••

YOU GET TO DECIDE
HOW YOU WANT TO
DEFINE YOURSELF
TO THE WORLD.

-- LIZZIE VELÁZQUEZ

ME, IN 50 WORDS OR LESS:

I don't say no
because I'm so busy.
I say no because I don't
want to be so busy.

-- Courtney Carver

THINGS I SUPPORT AND GIVE MY TIME TO:

THINGS I CHOOSE TO SAY 'NO' TO:

A SIMPLE LIFE IS ITS OWN REWARD.

-- GEORGE SANTAYANA

I COULD SIMPLIFY MY LIFE BY:

We're being
pulled in a thousand
different directions;
somehow, it's all
urgent, and it's
all important.

Decide where to put
your energy,
or the chaos will
decide for you.

-- Brooke Hampton

A SNAPSHOT OF MY ACTIVITIES:

IMPORTANT/ URGENT:	IMPORTANT/NOT URGENT:

NOT IMPORTANT/ URGENT:	NOT IMPORTANT/NOT URGENT:

Gratitude
makes sense of our past,
brings peace for today, and
creates a vision for tomorrow.

-- Melody Beattie

I AM GRATEFUL FOR...

DON'T WAIT.

THE TIME WILL NEVER BE JUST RIGHT.

-- NAPOLEON HILL

THINGS I HAVE BEEN WAITING FOR:

Ten years from now,
make sure you can
say that you chose
your life, you didn't
settle for it.

-- MANDY HALE

I CHOOSE...

ABUNDANCE BELONGS TO ME.

-- GABBY BERNSTEIN

A FULL AND ABUNDANT LIFE MEANS...

LIVE IN THE PRESENT,
AND MAKE IT SO BEAUTIFUL
IT WILL BE WORTH REMEMBERING.

-- IDA SCOTT TAYLOR

THINGS IN WHICH I SEE BEAUTY:

Success is not final,
failure is not fatal;
it is the courage
to continue that counts.

-- Winston Churchill

MY COURAGEOUS ACTS:

>>>——→

>>>——→

>>>——→

>>>——→

>>>——→

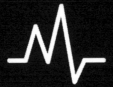

KNOWING HOW YOU
WANT TO FEEL
IS THE MOST POWERFUL
FORM OF CLARITY YOU CAN HAVE.

-- DANIELLE LAPORTE

I WANT TO FEEL MORE:

1

2

3

4

5

6

Decluttering is infinitely
easier when you think of it
as deciding what to keep,
rather than deciding
what to throw away.

-- Francine Jay

WHAT DO I WANT TO KEEP IN MY LIFE?

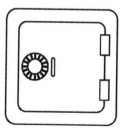

You can't go back
and change
the beginning,
but you can start
where you are and
change the ending.

-- C. S. Lewis

THINGS I WISH TO CHANGE...

The space in which
we LIVE should be
for the person we
are becoming NOW,
not for the person
we were in the PAST.

-- Marie Kondo

THE PERSON I AM BECOMING...

If you get out of your comfort zone
and embrace some discomfort,
it enables you to grow.

-- MICHAEL HYATT

AREAS I'D LIKE TO GROW:

MEMORIES AND MOMENTS
ARE OUR ONLY
SUSTAINABLE CURRENCY.

-- MILES ADCOX

MY FAVORITE MEMORIES:

Breathe, darling.

This is just a chapter.

It's not your whole story.

-- S.C. Lourie

THE TITLE OF MY LIFE'S STORY:

THIS CHAPTER WOULD BE CALLED:

• • •

THE BEST WAY
TO PREDICT
YOUR FUTURE
IS TO CREATE IT.

-- ABRAHAM LINCOLN

MY LIST OF FUTURE ACHIEVEMENTS:

ACKNOWLEDGMENTS

Many amazing people have supported me in my journey.

A special thank you to:

My husband, Robert, for your unconditional love, quiet encouragement, and sense of adventure; you have my heart.

My daughters, Addison and Lauren – our silly songs, belly laughs, and sweet hugs and kisses are among my favorite things. May you always dream big. Mama loves you.

My publisher, Demi Stevens, for your wisdom, guidance, and kind heart.

My community of thinkers, doers, and creatives – you inspire me to follow my dreams.

ABOUT THE AUTHOR

Katie Caples is a dreamer, learner, and encourager. She's a wife and mom of two beautiful daughters. A farm girl that savors mountain air and bluegrass music, she takes time to enjoy the simple things.

Her intent for this journal is self-reflection. After welcoming her second child, she was in search of an inspiring way to capture her thoughts and challenge her mind. When she couldn't find it, she created it, and rediscovered her passion for writing and design.

With more than ten years of experience in sales and management, Katie boldly transitioned from a career she loved with a community nonprofit organization to one of author and entrepreneur.

To learn more about her journey, visit her at kcaples.com.

74662669R00075

Made in the USA
Middletown, DE
29 May 2018